Let's Fight About Money

How to communicate about money, handle conflict and build an unbreakable financial house!

By: Martin & Chelsea Matthews

Cover Design: Ken Yonker & Samantha Ferrara

Acknowledgements

We would like to thank God for bringing us together and blessing our family in countless ways.

We would also like to thank our parents, Curt and Karen (Chelsea's Parents) and Gabriel, Helena and step-dad Joe (Martin's Parents).

Special Thanks to Joseph Giglietti for helping us through the process of becoming authors. Your insight has been invaluable.

To the mentors we've had throughout the years, thank you for pouring into us. We will continue to pour into others.

THANK YOU to everyone who supports us. Thanks for your kind words and loving hearts.

Dedicated To: Gabriel Baccus Matthews, Andrew Matthews and Steven Striker. Always in our hearts.

Comments

"Let's Fight About Money is an inspirational and priceless book filled with real life and practical lessons that any couple can use to navigate financial pitfalls.

A lot of couples fight and argue over money matters. Martin and Chelsea Matthews are experts in the field of finance and in this book, teach couples how to communicate and create a step by step plan to reach financial independence.

I will be recommending this book to my advisors and clients as a MUST READ!"

Daniel A. Kravitz
CEO-Founder of Millennial Property & Casualty Insurance. National Best-Selling Co-author, **Initiative**

"Martin and Chelsea have been so generous in helping my husband and I with a few of the essential building blocks of our finances.

Having all the proper things in place gives us peace of mind when it comes to financial security for our family. They've broken through all financial professionals do by combing relationships and how it relates to money on a daily basis."

Lisa Marie Kennedy
Luxury Real Estate Agent, Author of **Selling The Million Dollar Model**

Table of Contents

Chapter 1

Why Do People Fight About Money?

A few years ago, Chelsea and I took some close friends to a very nice restaurant for dinner. Before we went, we had a "general" agreement on how much we were going to spend that night. I say "general' because I wanted a little wiggle room. In my mind, I didn't entirely agree with the range she suggested, but I didn't want to argue about it. That was probably *Mistake Number 1*.

As we were sitting and chatting, I began thinking about the amazing burger I had there a few months prior, for my birthday. It was their flagship burger, and they even serve it with a little toothpick holding up the American flag. The more I thought about it, the more I started craving the burger, which also happened to be the most expensive item on the menu.

I wanted it really bad and thought, 'when it's time to order what I want to eat, I should get it and not settle for something else.' Budget? What budget? When I told Chelsea my response to 'So, what are you thinking about getting?" she didn't look happy that my choice would put us over budget. Why didn't she want me to enjoy this burger? Why?! From my perspective she was just trying to give me restrictions and wasn't being flexible.

Chelsea: We talked about this, but Martin wanted what he wanted and didn't want to compromise. We were treating our guests, and I wanted us to have a less expensive item so we could stay within our budget. He had that specific burger in mind and didn't want to have anything else. To me, not wanting to be flexible felt like he was saying our family and our guests weren't important. He wanted what he wanted, and the financial situation didn't matter because he wanted it. I just felt like he didn't care.

The burger incident was how some things started opening up for us about financial communication. He said, "When you're craving something, you should just get it because nothing else will satisfy and you'll just be upset that you **had** to get something else." While that might seem to make sense on the surface, getting whatever you want, whenever you want it, is rarely the answer for long term success.

Martin: As we discussed it, I started asking myself, "Why did I allow my desire for the meal to overpower my logic to stay within the budget? Why did I equate Chelsea's desire to remain on budget, generally something good, to mean she wanted to deny me something? Where did the belief that I deserved the burger no matter what, come from?

I think that view came from growing up in a poor, war-torn African country. In my home country, Liberia, there were times when you had to eat whatever you could find. During the war, there were no luxuries. We barely had the basics regarding food. There was a time when I couldn't even dream of eating a burger.

My experience of being denied during the war led me to believe that nothing should stop me from getting this. I felt like I deserved it. How many times have you felt that way, especially if you work hard?

Essentially, I communicated to Chelsea that I didn't care what it cost; I wanted it because I wanted it. Internally I was simply thinking about when I couldn't even come close to having a burger. So, even if it wasn't in the budget, if I wanted this burger, I was going to have it. How many times have you gone over budget to get something you truly want? If you're like me, there's been a few.

So, something as simple as a burger created an issue of conflict. The burger didn't cause the conflict, though. In fact, it wasn't even about the burger; it was our different perspectives clashing that caused the conflict.

Money is the number one thing people fight and argue about, and the number one cause of divorce.

When we started applying the principles we learned from years of personal development to our conflicts about money; we cracked the code to understanding WHY people fight about money, HOW to fight fair and then actually ENJOY money conversations.

This book will show you a simple and clear approach to help you solve conflicts in this area, and we believe you can use this same method in other areas of your life.

Because of this incident, Chelsea and I ended up starting a discussion to understand each other's perspectives. We knew we simply saw things differently and we could address that.

Chelsea: No one fights because they have too much money. It's usually the opposite. There's often not enough. People have too many expenses and too few dollars. When you add misunderstandings and miscommunications to that mix, you get conflicts that can be difficult to solve.

We believe this is particularly the case when it comes to money and relationships. One person may be a spender and the other a saver. They often don't know what their money beliefs or habits are, so they argue because the other person has different beliefs and habits. They don't understand why they disagree. They see things from their perspective like I did with the burger Martin wanted.

Ultimately, we have to balance all the things we need and want with the limited amount of resources we have. And since Men and Women are wired differently, we don't always agree on how to use our resources.

If one person is a spender and wants to spend on something while the other person is a saver, the saver gets stressed out or worried.

They think the spender is not being responsible or thinking about the family. The spender thinks the saver doesn't trust them or worse, acts as a parent always telling them NO. They may not even know exactly why they feel threatened, they just know the stressful feeling it creates, and they don't understand where the other person is coming from.

Martin: So, whose fault is it? No one is taught how to communicate about money. Your parents likely weren't taught, and so, they didn't know how to show you. It's not taught in schools, and many people don't even know what needs to change let alone how to change the situation.

In our society today, we have so many demands on our resources. Within that environment, there's always going to be some conflict around money. Even if you resolve to:

A) Make more money.

B) Reduce your expenses to fit the amount you have.

Conflict will arise at some point. Since there will always be conflict, it's crucial how you handle it. The reality is, even successful people are facing pressure in the area of their finances and conflicts keep happening. They haven't learned to deal with it, and that's part of why they fight.

Since we learn so much from our parents, it's important to look back and consider how they handled their conflicts about money.

Chelsea: Growing up, I didn't really see my parents fight at all. When they divorced, my mom struggled financially. She worked a job and even had her own side business making fitness clothing. I thought she loved it, but later I found out that she only did it because she was good at it and needed the money.

We moved from the large and beautiful custom home I grew up in, to a teeny tiny little house where my bedroom was the screened in porch that barely fit my bed. Then she got remarried, and we moved into a beautiful big house again.

It seemed like my mom struggled on her own and felt like she needed to have a man to have financial security. But, she ended up getting taken advantage of. She worked hard and saved $50,000. When she got remarried, it seemed like there would be more financial security, but she ended up getting convinced to use all her savings for her new husband's construction business. The investment went under, and he lost the money, with no plan to replace it. It was just gone!

I don't remember them fighting about money specifically; they just seemed to fight about everything. Looking back, I'm sure money played a significant role in the arguments. When they divorced, we moved into another tiny house, and my mom struggled again. She worked hard after having to start all over. She had to build her savings and repair her credit which had taken a major hit too.

From my mom's perspective, money was hard to make, and it could leave you, or you could get taken advantage of by men, and they shouldn't be trusted. From my dad and my stepdad, I saw them build their businesses and somehow they always made it work and seemed to be just fine, while my mom always seemed to struggle in survival mode. She always made things work, and we had what we needed, but it just seemed to be a struggle.

Martin: As we peel back the layers of why people fight about money, we also see that it has to do with the beliefs they have created or built up over time. For example, if someone borrowed money and never paid it back, or worse, stole from you; it could create the belief that you can't trust people when it comes to money.

Chelsea: Here's what I learned: I felt like I struggled to make money even though I worked hard. I would try to save it, and then I would get into these relationships where I would pay for everything. My money would just seem to go away. What I saw, unconsciously I repeated.

Martin: In my case, my parents never really fought about money, but my mom was always dependent on my father financially. There wasn't anything to fight about because he provided it and she received it.

There were times when my mom and I had some conflict around money as a child because she would sometimes ask me for money. I felt like as the parent she was supposed to be the one helping me with money, not me giving her money because she was the adult.

So, I would say "no." And she would say "Why do you have to be so mean?" Maybe she was joking, or maybe that was the belief she had when it came to money; that it was up to someone else to provide for her.

Money has so much emotion tied to it that conflicts stem from people's beliefs and their experiences around money, which has led them to those beliefs. So, it's not only that they are fighting about it because they disagree in the present. It's that their beliefs, even before they begin the relationship, have been shaped.

It's almost like they are converging and eventually a conflict will arise. These two different people, with different beliefs, formed by their past experiences, will eventually disagree on how to best use limited resources. That's even more complicated by the fact that they have probably never talked about or have even been aware of their money beliefs.

No one begins the relationship by saying, "Hey, by the way, this is what I believe about money…This is where it comes from…This is what I saw my parents do…This is what someone else did to me…and now those are my money beliefs. What about you? What are your beliefs and why?"

If you never discuss your money beliefs, you eventually end up butting heads and sooner or later they collide, leading to a fight.

So, what's an example when I wanted to spend money and you wanted to save money? Let's talk about how we dealt with that conflict.

Chelsea: This was an area we had to navigate through and communicate a lot about because I had these fears of someone taking advantage of me. The fact that Martin was a spender terrified me when it came to combining our money, because that meant that I would have to give up having total control over it.

Well, I'll tell you another time that goes to fears I had from past relationships and experiences. One day before we were married or combined our money, Martin took my car to put gas in it for me. I gave him my card with a specific amount of $30, but instead, he filled it up for $75, and I freaked out. That was NOT the amount I said! For me, that was confirmation that "See, I can't trust him with my money. I can't combine my money because see...there it is. I gave him a chance, and he blew it."

Those words may sound irrational, but as we've mentioned, we often behave emotionally when it comes to money. It's almost like when someone has been cheated on and then doesn't fully trust a new person. That new person hasn't done anything to them, but their fears of repeating past mistakes can often be hard to ignore.

When you think about it, Martin wasn't going and blowing money at the casino. That may have been more than I had budgeted for gas, but he likes to have a full tank of gas because he doesn't want us to get stranded anywhere. It's a safety thing.

So for him, he was trying to protect us by filling up the gas tank. But to me, I was using that as confirmation that I couldn't trust him to combine our money. I felt I would be stupid to let the past repeat itself.

Martin: Okay, that's a great point right there as to where the conflict comes from because, in reality, it wasn't a real conflict. I thought I was doing something good. It all comes from a good place. You coming from a good place of "I want to make sure things are within the budget." I'm coming from a good place of "I wouldn't want you to be driving out oneday and run out of gas and be stuck in the middle of somewhere."

We are all trying to do something good for our family. She wanted to make sure the family sticks within the budget and I wanted to ensure that if an emergency happens, we aren't stuck somewhere out of gas. But, the conflict came from our perception of it. She perceived it one way, and I perceived it another. It's the same thing with the burger. It has to do with our perception and our interpretation of what's going on.

Chelsea: And that's how it gets so deep seeded because each person is coming from their perspective and they are coming from a good place with a good intention, and it's confusing like "why is this person mad at me for trying to do this good thing? I might as well not even try. We just won't talk about it, or we argue about it."
That's why people get so angry because they are coming from a good place and they feel attacked by their partner.

Martin: Communicating how a particular action feels emotionally, even if it makes no sense, is a good start. Putting extra gas in the car was something done with good intentions, but I was showing that I was a spender. Even though Chelsea was conscious about the budget, to her, my actions equated that I can't be trusted with money. Even though it may not logically make sense at the time, it is valid because the person feels it.

Action to take:

1. What was your experience with money growing up?

2. What did you hear people say about money?

3. How do you think this has affected your money beliefs today?

Take the time to answer each question for yourself and then without judgment, share your answers with each other.

For additional resources to help you on your journey, visit: **LetsFightAboutMoney.Com**

Chapter 2

Do We Still Need to Talk About it If One Person Handles The Money?

Some time ago Chelsea and I heard a very successful businessman say publicly how bad his wife is with money. He said it was so bad that they kept separate bank accounts and she always blew through hers. He also mentioned how they don't talk about money because it always ended in an argument. This shows that even people who are financially successful avoid talking about money if there may be some conflict involved.

Chelsea: I was very surprised by what this man said. He and his wife are an awesome couple. They're very generous, and while I'm sure he's willing to address issues in his business, he didn't want to address this particular issue with his wife. One reason could be he simply did not know HOW to address it to move from a conflict to a resolution. When we don't know HOW to do something, especially if dealing with it could be unpleasant, we tend to avoid it. Or we tend to slap a Band-Aid on it and move on.

Imagine if you had a business partner who continually went over budget when buying supplies. Would you say to them, "from now on, I'll put money into your bank account, and you can spend it however you want"? OR would you discuss what the business should be spending money on and why it's important to minimize expenses to keep the company profitable?

Every good business person addresses money issues, yet it seems a bit harder when it comes to personal relationships.

Martin: As licensed financial professionals, when we meet with our clients to help them plan for their future, one of the biggest obstacles we encounter is that one spouse knows what's happening with the finances and the other has very little idea.

One spouse handling things may work for a while, but if anything happened to them or the marriage ended in a divorce, the one who wasn't as involved ends up struggling to adjust since their spouse is no longer handling things for them.

We knew someone whose husband managed all the financial affairs. He kept detailed records in a box and was very organized. After he had passed away, his wife spent nearly a year staring at the closed box of their financial records.

For almost an entire year, she couldn't bring herself to open the box. She was terrified and didn't know what to do or even where to start. Her husband rarely talked to her about their money. They were pretty well off and just avoided discussing it. Even if one person primarily handles the finances, they both need to talk and understand what's going on.

Action to take:

1. Schedule a weekly time to meet and discuss your family finances and goals.

2. Make sure you both know about all existing accounts and have access to them.

For more resources and accountability go to: **LetsFightAboutMoney.com**

Chapter 3

You say To-MAY-To, and I say To-MAH-To: How Your Money Personality Affects Your Relationship & What to Do about It

Martin: After a couple of years being in America, I ended up in Minnesota working at a department store in the country's largest mall. Mall of America had everything, tons of stores, a movie theater and even an indoor roller coaster! I was legally an adult with a job but had never learned any money management skills.

Whenever my bank account reached over a certain amount, I would have a burning desire to spend my money. I remember walking through the mall literally looking for something to buy, even if I didn't have anything specific in mind. I felt good walking through the mall with bags in hand.

Since we know that money conflicts arise because we have different habits, beliefs, and perspectives, we need to know what our money personality is. Personality refers to individual differences in patterns of thinking, feeling and behaving. How we think, feel and behave with money is our money personality. My money personality is a spender. Here's an explanation of each one:

Money Personalities

1. Saver/Hoarder (of everything including energy)

This is a form of control. Savers see savings as building up a buffer of protection. They are often described as responsible, and they're proud of what they save.

They'll reconcile bank statements to the penny each month. They tend to check their bills twice and are often in fear of not having money.

2. Spender (of everything including energy)

They often use spending as an emotional scapegoat. It's not just about releasing money but the emotions, "retail therapy" and good feelings that come with spending money.

The word **responsible** makes them feel sick to their stomach. They just assume bank statements & bills are right & super easy to add up because there's nothing left. They're too comfortable with the word overdraft and tend to put off saving.

They often have lots of friends who love to go out and let them pay the bill & they're more than happy to pay. They spend for approval and often live way above their means.

3. Avoider

An avoider doesn't open their bills. Their mascot is an ostrich since they bury their head in the sand & hope the topic goes away!

They may even have everything neatly organized but unopened. They also don't check bills; they just assume it's right and usually tend to avoid responsibility.

4. Money Monk

They believe money & spirituality don't mix and that money is beneath them. They're fond of saying how little they care about money.

Some people will lose money & believe they will get brownie points morally.

5. Amasser

They are happiest when they have large amounts of money at their disposal to spend, to save, and to invest. If they're not spending, saving, or investing, they may feel empty or not fully alive.

They tend to equate money with self-worth and power, so a lack of money may lead to feelings of failure and even depression. If they hire an investment advisor or financial planner, their primary concern will be finding investments with high rates of return, since they hope to make as much money as they can, as quickly as possible.

If that sounds like you and you tend to be a worrier, as well as tired of being overly obsessed with your money, you may welcome the opportunity to assign some of the details of your money to a trustworthy financial advisor.

Chelsea: With me being a fearful saver, Martin would feel like I was trying to tell him what he could or couldn't spend money on and he felt like I wanted to control him. I was worried about spending and felt like he would spend all the money for stuff he wanted without discussing it, even if it were things for us or our business. But, once we were able to identify that Martin was a spender and I was a saver, we could understand where each other was coming from and stop blaming.

I now know and can appreciate that I tend to think from scarcity and wanting to save with a fear of spending. I began to see that I probably could be a little more open minded and if I feel fearful of spending in a particular area I can ask myself these three questions…

1. What am I actually afraid of?

2. Is it really dangerous for us?

3. Is it coming up because it's my money personality or reminds me of a past experience?

 Just by asking myself those questions, I can usually reach a conclusion if my thoughts are valid or coming from an unsupportive belief.

The same goes for Martin; he asks himself these three questions:

1. Why do I want to spend on this particular thing?

2. Is it something we actually need?

3. Am I spending out of rebellion to show that I can do what I want with money?

Martin: Here's an example of how we've both been able to compromise and find a good solution. We were looking at purchasing a course that would fill a knowledge gap in something we were working on. The course was initially offered at a steep discount and we had missed it. When we went to make the purchase, the price has gone up to $1,000. I suggested we see if we could still get it for a special price.

Chelsea: We knew the person and came up with some other ways we could add value to them. We asked for the deal we missed, and we got it! So this is a great example of how he's evolved in thinking more like a saver and how we can both consider each other's money personalities when making money decisions.

We identify if our feelings are valid or just a response from our beliefs, then we decide together if we spend or not.

Martin encouraged me to open myself up to the kind of spending that allows us to expand our business, grow and to think from a more abundant frame of mind. Instead of always being worried that money is going to leave us, I practice thinking about money coming to us easily.

I have encouraged him to think more about the things he wants to spend money on and if it's something that will help us grow, if it's something that we need, or if we will be overextending ourselves. So we have helped each other balance out a little bit and come together in the middle.

So, what is your money personality?

Action to take:

1. What is your money personality?

2. How has that served you in a positive way?

3. How has that affected you in a negative way?

Take the time to answer each question for yourself and then without judgment, share your answers with each other.

For more resources and accountability go to: **LetsFightAboutMoney.com**

Chapter 4

Why I Couldn't Find the Cause Until I Looked In The Mirror: How Self Reflection Can Lead to Self-Correction

Martin: As we've pointed out, I'm a spender, especially when it comes to growing our business. A few years ago some very expensive software came out that I felt would help our business in a major way. I was dazzled by what it could do, and since there wasn't a trial version, I had to get my hands on the full software. I wanted to be one of the first in a new wave of people to get this new and improved version. It was a major decision and source of tension in our relationship as I was pushing Chelsea for us to make this purchase and we weren't even married yet. Ultimately, we spent several thousand dollars on this software and even traveled across the country to learn how to use it.

Had I truly thought about it, I would have realized this software would not spark the business growth I wanted and might even create problems. In our business as licensed financial professionals, Chelsea and I not only work with clients, but we train and mentor other independent financial educators. Not everyone could afford to spend that much on software. Our business relies on consistency, and if some people had the software and others didn't, some would get left behind.

I should have realized that most people would not spend that much money and shouldn't have tried to move so quickly on it. In my excitement to grow and expand rapidly, I pushed Chelsea to get involved and help make the investment. That's when I started to look in the mirror at what I was spending money on and if it was the best use of it. I realized I needed to start thinking a little more before spending money, even if I thought spending would improve the business or lead to more money. It's about becoming more practical and rational versus being emotional.

Chelsea: That's a good example because where that money came from was not for spending in the business. That's probably where the fear started coming up when I felt like I was repeating my past experiences. That money, in particular, came from child support that I had received after years of not getting anything.

At the time, I felt extremely pressured by Martin, if I didn't do it that I was not all in on the relationship or the business we were building. It was a reminder of the way I was often pressured in a past relationship. I felt very conflicted because I felt like this was money I had been waiting seven years to get and as soon as I get it, a guy talks me into spending it. It made me start to feel fearful of even having money because I feared the conflict of being pressured to spend it.

This chapter is about taking responsibility. Even if you have a spouse who doesn't want to participate, isn't willing to look at their role, or just won't communicate...you can still look in the mirror and figure out your beliefs and what you can do to change them.

The experience I had with bad relationships, guys taking advantage of me and my money caused me to believe that I was choosing all the wrong guys…and I was really good at it. I believed I was a poor judge of character; I even had a friend tell me that. I just thought I was a jerk magnet. But, when I started thinking about the relationship my mom had with my stepdad and what I learned about money through her experiences…I realized it was almost identical to the relationships I kept finding myself in.

It was like a lightbulb switched on, and I realized how much what I saw growing up had shaped my beliefs, and I just repeated it. It was my choice, unconsciously because of my beliefs about money that guys take advantage of me. That's when I started looking in the mirror and asking myself what kind of person I wanted in my and William's life. Then, I knew who I had to become…the kind of person that would attract this sort of man. So, I started doing the work to change my beliefs and actions and ultimately my habits. Shortly after that is when Martin and I met.

I thought it was them, outside of my control. But, it was the beliefs inside of me that attracted those relationships.

Martin: When I had money, one of the ways I mismanaged my funds, you could say, is when a family member needed money. I would often send it to them. I expected they would do the same thing for me, and I felt like they had to, why wouldn't they? "I've given you some money, why couldn't you give me some money if I'm going through a tough time?"

I started to realize that I was responsible for myself and that other people were not going to be responsible for me. I began to look at it critically and thought I did need to manage my money better.

Even though it may have meant I had to give less, spend less or do fewer things, I could be better with the resources I had. Because, after going through some tough times some of the family members I helped did not reach out to help me. Even friends I had helped told me they weren't in a position to do anything. Giving is still important to me, so today when I help family members, I don't expect anything in return. I just give what I can.

We all have to look in the mirror. All of us are where we are financially because of the decisions we've made. You may have made them because of your money personality, because of what you observed or even because you just never learned about money.

Once you become aware of your beliefs and accept your money personality you can detach from the limiting beliefs and change your habits.

Here are some basic observations to help you start the conversation. From what we've seen, women tend to stick closer to the budget and the men tend to be the ones who want to buy the big toys and overspend. The wife doesn't want to tell her husband what to do, but may also be afraid of having money available because the guy might want to spend it, especially if he's a spender.

Chelsea: That reminds me of something from a past relationship. In that relationship, the person liked gambling, and I would have to hide money, so it didn't get gambled. With Martin, his spending was harder to recognize, because he wasn't out gambling or spending frivolously. The things he wanted to spend on, except food ;) is usually to grow our business. He's a risk taker and likes to test things. Even if he doesn't know whether it will work out, he likes to try things out, and that's a little scary for me. I want to know we have a good chance to succeed at something we are investing in, especially if it's not just extra money that we have to spend. So, it's harder to identify it because he's coming from a good place. If guys are out spending a bunch of money on gambling and drinking, it's much easier to identify because those things aren't bettering your life or business.

It's very hard to look into the mirror and ask myself if the fear I am feeling is coming from a past experience or from something that's going on right now. It's hard because it feels very real and very current. Even in the specific stories we have shared, there are things that we needed to talk about and come to an agreement and understand why we felt the way we did.

It was extremely scary for me because I felt like if I recognized or admitted that maybe some of these beliefs were coming from fears of past experiences, did that mean that I had to let go of the current fear I was feeling? Did that mean I was wrong? Did that mean I'm just supposed to let him be right when it comes to spending?

It was tough to admit that some of my fears were not valid in our current situation because that would mean I had to let go of some of it. Did that also mean I had to be vulnerable, open myself to the risk of someone else taking advantage of me?

Self-reflection is a major part of money communication.

Martin: Since women are more likely to be the ones leading this conversation, a great place to start in helping your partner look in the mirror is to help them understand their money personality and what their money beliefs are.

Imagine them saying, 'Wow I'm looking in the mirror and I'm seeing what I'm doing.' I think what's happening is they aren't seeing what they are doing that's causing the conflict or allowing the conflict to fester. Until they look at it and say, I've recognized that how I was behaving or misbehaving led to this fear and because of this person's money beliefs based on their past experiences or based on what they saw in life is affecting this relationship today.

Action to take:

1. What are some areas in your relationship that you have conflicts about money?

2. Think of a specific example: What happened?

3. How did you feel about it?

4. What did it mean or communicate to you?

5. Can you think of an experience in your past that may be similar to this one?

6. Is it possible that a previous experience may have played a role in your thoughts about this event?

Take the time to answer each question for yourself and then without judgment, share your answers with each other...It doesn't have to be the same incident.

For more resources and accountability go to:
LetsFightAboutMoney.com

Chapter 5

Put Down The Gloves:
How To Become Closer by Fighting The Right Way

Chelsea: To properly handle conflict, communication is critical. When it comes to the battle of the sexes, women will most likely be the savers and the ones with spending fears. So, I would say the best place to come from is to first work on yourself. Get clear about what your beliefs are and where they came from. Are they serving you? If not, what kind of beliefs would help you?

Women are also more likely to be the ones starting the conversation about money. Ladies, when you talk with your spouse, especially if it has to do with their spending, the biggest thing to remember is that men don't want to feel like their wives are telling them what to do, especially when it comes to money. They want to feel like the provider and feel like they're in charge of the family, like they are the protector.

We believe the more you can communicate about how something makes you feel, the more likely you are to resolve a conflict. Here's a simple formula we call the **ABCs of Money Communication.**

A ---------------------→ B ---------------------→ C --------- ---------------- = Success

A. In Specific Situation →B. When You Do This →C. It Makes Me Feel

For example:

A. In trying to grow our business
B. When you spend money without letting me know
C. It makes me feel afraid and not considered in that decision.

Or:

A. During times that you're out shopping
B. When you apply for a store credit card
C. It makes me feel unimportant that you didn't include me in something that affects our family's finances.

Or:

A. In handling the budget
B. When you ask me about every single transaction
C. It makes me feel like a child whose mother has to check on everything he does.

[**Note**: It's not enough to just help with communication, chapter eight will cover financial concepts to start you down the path of a spending plan so you can have guilt-free spending where you'll be free to spend some of your money however you want! Visit: **Webinar.FinancialLiteracyMatters.com** to watch our FREE webinar about it.]

You also have to do the WORK. Throughout this book, we've been building towards your understanding of these two formulas: the **ABCs of Money Communication** and **WORK.**

W = Win-Win

O = Ownership

R = Respect Each Other

K = Keep The Big Picture In Mind

W = Win-Win: Fighting with your spouse about money or any other issue is about fighting fair. It's not about winning. It's about creating a win-win. It's about listening and working together so the both of you can move forward with a stronger relationship. If your spouse does not feel heard, you have NOT created a win-win. We'll share some practical rules on fighting to create a win-win.

O = Ownership: You must take ownership for your part in everything. The chapter on looking in the mirror was to help you understand the importance of accepting responsibility.

R = Respect Each Other: To understand and deal with money conflicts you must listen to and respect your partner. Learn to put yourself in their shoes

K = Keep the Big Picture in Mind: You've been handling money your entire life, and you'll continue to handling money. You should keep the big picture of your family, financial security and ultimately financial freedom in mind.

Martin: We began this book uncovering where the conflict in relationships come from. By understanding how we're all different, you can start to see where your partner is coming from and then you start taking responsibility for your role. In my case, I put on the armor of a spender and fully accepted it. Once you do this for yourself, you can start working towards changing your beliefs. You cannot change what you're not aware of. Accepting your beliefs makes it easier to understand your partner.

There's another layer of looking in the mirror. As men, we want to protect and take care of our family and that's why many of us work so hard. We don't realize that some of the things we do actually make our partner feel less protected.

For example, my spending would be making Chelsea feel less protected and more afraid. Until you look in the mirror and realize that, it's harder for you to say "Wow, ok let me curb this behavior because it displays to my partner that I'm not being considerate or protective or the provider I really want to be." So, you want to make sure that you're accepting of what they say. You should have an agreement that whenever these types of feelings come up that you both will discuss it in a positive way.

Before we get into some specific rules of fighting fair, here are the overall DONT'S. Don't **DUCK**…. You can't run, hide or avoid.

D = Defensive

U = Undermine

C = Criticize

K = Know It All

D = Defensive: Don't get defensive and don't make excuses. Listen to your partner and remember that what they are saying may be coming from a money belief or past experience. However, this is not the time to tell them that. Try to be open to the role that you could be playing in the issue your partner is communicating. This does not mean that you are admitting any fault, but you are willing to listen and consider what is being said. Try to put yourself in your partner's shoes and see if you can understand where they may be coming from.

U = Undermine: Never, ever undermine your relationship. If you have children, DO NOT have money fights around them. Why? Think of your money beliefs and where they came from. If some of them came from your parents and what they did or how they fought about money, you don't want to transmit that to your kids. You can teach your kids money lessons, and we will get to that in the coming chapters. But you don't want to have those discussions with children around. If they are little, wait until they go to sleep or wait until you can talk privately.

NEVER have money fights in public!

Chelsea: If you're in public and have to address it right then, send a text. Whenever Martin and I had a difference of opinion and our son William was in the room, I would just send a text message. With that method, you're not arguing in front of anyone but are able to get it off your mind. You can then move on until you can talk further when both of you can focus, listen and are in the right frame of mind. Remember the **ABCs of Money Communication:**

A. <u>In (Specific) Situation</u>
B. <u>When You Do (X)</u>
C. <u>It Makes Me Feel (Y)</u>

Another option is to take some time and write down the feelings or issue you have to get clear about your thoughts. Another reason I would text Martin is that sometimes I can be very blunt and it can come across unpleasantly. So, I might just say "I don't want to spend on this" or "This is over the budget" and it may come across harsh. So, I would write out what I wanted to say, and I still do sometimes. I would write it out, then read it to myself and see if it's something I would want to say when I'm in a good state of mind. If I'm upset about something, I often write it down and wait until I'm not upset to see if I really need to communicate it and if it's going to communicate what I want.

C = Criticize: Whenever you criticize, the other person can get defensive. When one person gets defensive, it's not easy to come to a resolution. The easiest way to prevent that is to avoid criticism.

If there is something you must address, be sure it's an appropriate time when both of you can focus on the discussion and always start with something positive. Your partner is more likely to be open to hearing what you have to say if you balance it with pointing out something they do well.

K = Know It All: Don't jump to a conclusion or act like you know what the other person is trying to say. Make sure to listen, so you actually hear them.

Here are a few additional examples of communication to avoid. Saying things like: *"You spent money on that stupid boat"* or *"You don't even use those golf clubs, why did you waste that money"*, you could say *"In this situation...this is how I feel..."*

Communicate where your feelings are coming from, if you know. This will take the blame away from your partner.

I have been taken advantage of in past relationships, so the feelings I may have about a situation, may not be directly related to Martin but could be coming from a past experience. That's one thing I have learned to communicate with Martin.

I say, *"I'm not sure if this is coming from a past experience, but this is how I'm feeling."* Or *"I feel scared when you want to spend on this...because I worry that every time we have money, it's going to go away."*

That way it takes the blame away from "he's doing it to me" and giving a little slack and saying "hey, maybe this is my own issue and I have to communicate it. This isn't saying that no one does any wrong or you have to take the blame for everything. It's just another way to consider where your reaction may be coming from and by approaching it this way, your partner is more open to hearing what you have to say because they don't feel like they have to defend themselves.

Martin: Sometimes if you need to communicate something that is affecting your mood and you just can't get beyond it or put it aside then you want to use that texting method. It's a quick way to let them know "Hey, this is coming up for me and I just want to let you know." Sometimes we may not be aware of what we're doing, and it can let us know to adjust something or discuss the matter later.

The main thing is to fight the right fight. Families don't want to fight each other; they want to fight FOR each other. You want to understand how to communicate well with each other. Then you want to get all your differences and put them on the same page.

Today, one of the ways I fight for my family is to look for ways that we can find good deals. If I really want to buy something, I start to think "Is there a way to make it more cost effective? Is there a different way to do this and get the same outcome? The more you think about it, the more considerate you become as you fight for your family's financial future.

Sit with your family and create joint family goals. Talk about where you want to go as a family, as a couple and then work towards that collectively. You may say "I know I'm a spender, so I'm going to curb it and meet my partner in the middle." The other person may say "Well, I know I tend to be a saver and I want to hold on to the money, but I can be a little more open to the things you want to do."

Now that you both understand where you're coming from as a family and as a couple, you can be confident you're heading in the right direction. When conflict arises, because you and your partner understand each other's money beliefs, you will communicate with care and consideration when discussing issues.

You come together and meet in the middle because first, financial security is vital to feel safe and secure with your finances. Then financial freedom, so you can be free to live the life you want and not worry about money.

Your partner may be open to considering what part they could be playing in the conflict as well. The more you can take responsibility for your feelings and emotions, communicate how you feel and recognize it might be coming from something in the past, the more you leave an opening for your partner to be receptive.

Even when you start making progress with your financial communication, another area to keep in mind is what kind of lifestyle you truly want to live. Sometimes one person believes their lifestyle should be at a certain amount and another person thinks it should be more or less.

As couples, we need to agree on what kind of lifestyle we want. How much money does it take? Can we do it efficiently for less? Then, you start having a general idea of how much money you need to generate every month. Once you know the amount, you can create a plan for your lifestyle. Then begin working together instead of working against each other to reach your financial goals. Until you know what kind of lifestyle you want and how much it's going to cost, it's hard to achieve it and become financially free.

Chelsea: If you don't want the same lifestyle and you don't have each other's best interest at heart, that's a whole other story. Then you must look at your relationship because families usually want the best for each other, and they want to live their best lives. If you can at least agree on that, then there is room to move forward together. But if you can't even agree on that, then you may consider professional counseling.

Martin: Yes, you might have more than just conflict around money. There could be deeper issues. For example, if I refused to look in the mirror and admit to being a spender and be willing to take responsibility for the effect it was having on Chelsea then we'd have to look at the whole relationship.

If I couldn't move beyond that, it would mean that my tendency to spend was being prioritized over her fear of running out of money. So that could mean there's something deeper that you both would need to work on.

Will this person adjust? It doesn't mean you must change everything about yourself. I still have the tendency to want to spend on things to expand our business, but I will first be more considerate about where we are spending our money and where it goes instead of just spending frivolously or openly as I did before.

Chelsea: You have to be willing to have the uncomfortable conversations. Just because you care about each other and you want the best for each other, and you have the same goals as each other doesn't mean that it's going to be easy. We still have some uncomfortable conversations sometimes. But, we know that we are going to come to a place that is a win-win.

I remember the conversation at the restaurant about what Martin wanted to order and to me, I could only see it my way and he could only see it his way. It may seem small by itself if we couldn't understand where each other was coming from, it could be a serious issue in our relationship. We had to be willing to go through the uncomfortableness of communicating until we could come to an understanding.

You have got to commit to it. You have got to be willing to do the WORK, it is SOOO worth it. If you do it and hang in there, it's not about getting the other person to agree with you. Sometimes we don't agree with each other, but it's about listening, respecting, no judgment and coming to a conclusion that's best for the family.

Martin: Even if you know how to do all these things effectively, you may still have ups and downs in your financial world. You could have a lot and then not. But, because you know how to effectively deal with these things you can still have peace financially.

So, it's not just conflict, you're not just fighting because now you understand how to deal with the fears that might come up. You have to be committed to doing it. Otherwise, it's not going to work. You have to be committed to discussing how you feel versus pointing fingers. If you aren't committed to adjusting your money behavior or letting go of past experiences, then you will NEVER resolve conflict around money or make the big picture work for you and your family.

Chelsea: It just made me think how we have been able to work together so well and communicate about money in such a short time. We had a very accelerated relationship from the time we met, we both were in the same business together, you jumped into being a dad to a 7-year-old, and then we moved across the country. We have been through ups and downs, parted ways with business partners, moved several times, built our business together, expanded our business together and got married all in just a few short years.

We have done more than some couples do in their entire life. That really was a test of our relationship. If you can pull together in the difficult, challenging times and come out thriving on the other side, then you know that you are built to last.

We spend an extraordinary amount of time together and that could have driven us apart really fast, and we could have driven each other crazy, but instead it has forced us to have the difficult conversations and figure out solutions to work together.

Martin: Families will always have some conflict on some level because we are human beings and don't always see things the same way. No matter how much you love each other, there will be some conflict. But, it is how you deal with the conflict, how you communicate about it and how you resolve it that will make your family stronger or weaker.

If you learn all these things and put them into place, conflicts will still arise. But you will have the tools to handle them.

As Chelsea said, we don't always agree with each other, but we have learned how to communicate based on our different money beliefs. Our desire is to make our family stronger and we are willing to make adjustments. For you to be successful as a family, especially when it comes to your resources which is the foundation of so much that you are going to do in your life, you have to be willing to do those things as well.

Action to take:

1. Apply the **ABCs of Money Communication** to a conflict you've had recently in your relationship.

2. How do you think it could have impacted the outcome if it was applied at the time of the conflict?

3. In what areas of **WORK** are you successfully using in your relationship?

4. What areas of **WORK** could you improve on?

5. Are there any areas in your relationship that you **DUCK**?

Take the time to answer each question for yourself and then without judgment, share your answers with each other.

If you need to, review the chapter to be sure you fully understand the meaning of the words in bold.

For more resources and accountability go to: LetsFightAboutMoney.com

Chapter 6:

Emotional Needs: Money and Sex

Chelsea: In our relationship we now have great communication and have worked through a lot of things, but that doesn't mean we don't ever have conflict. We don't just get along all the time. We look at things differently, experience things differently and we had a major disagreement about something in particular. There are two areas that couples fight about the most.

Generally men have one top emotional need, which we will get into in a minute. But first, let's talk about the ladies and their needs. Sometimes we talk to our husbands and try to tell them about our emotional needs. We may say things like "I want your undivided attention, your affection, family time." Men may wonder what that actually means. Sometimes it's hard to put these things into words.

So, I started researching emotional needs to find out exactly what mine were and how to communicate them. I came across an emotional needs questionnaire. There are 10 emotional needs most people have and the order of importance is unique to each person. I took the quiz and figured out what my top emotional needs were. Then I sent it to Martin and asked him to take the quiz and tell me what his top emotional needs were in order.

Martin: So I'm upstairs, she's downstairs and she sends me this thing asking me to take this little quiz. So I'm like, "Ok…here we go with the little quizzes again." So, I take the little quiz…

Chelsea: "You like taking little quizzes, don't you?"

Martin: "Yeah, but not the relationship ones." But tell them, what was the result?

Chelsea: Well, I love taking these kinds of quizzes. Ok, so the top four out of five were the same for us, maybe not the exact same order but the same needs. My top emotional need is financial security. ..and what is your top need?

Martin: My number one top emotional need is sexual fulfillment. This is number one, top of the list, beyond financial security, beyond everything else on the list.

Chelsea: Above affection, respect, honesty! He doesn't care if I lie to him as long as I take care of his top emotional need.

Martin: Lying could be saying "You are the best in the world." If you tell him that, even if it's not true…he's gonna think he's freaking Superman. He wants to hear that.

Chelsea: I think of lying as like cheating. I have learned that this top need is true for most men. I thought he was just a pervert. And let me tell you this, that need wasn't even in my top five.

Martin: Look, let me tell you where this need fell. Can you guess?

Chelsea: People are going to feel really sorry for you.

Martin: They aren't going to feel sorry for me because it's something we are all working through. Every guy understands this, it's the truth alright.

Chelsea: So, there's a list of 10 emotional needs and Martin sent me his top five. I asked him for the rest of his list, all 10 needs in order. I asked him this for a very specific reason. Sexual fulfillment did not even make my top five. It's not just about putting the needs in order. You have to go through each need and ask yourself if you could only have one and not the other, which would you choose.

For example, if you had to choose between sexual fulfillment or financial security…which would you choose? So, for me I thought physical attraction would be at the top of the list for me. But, when I had to pick one or the other and it came to things like honesty or physical attraction…honesty won along with many other needs. This is not true for all women, we are not all the same…but I would say this is definitely the majority of women.

Martin: Here's the deal, if sexual fulfillment is number one on my list and it's ten on her list…would you guys agree that we have a major disagreement?

Chelsea: Did you just tell them what number it is on my list?

Martin: I think I said it, but we can tell them now. We can say it.

Chelsea: Yes. It came in at number ten.

Martin: I wanted to run downstairs and say "What the heck?"

Chelsea: If I had to choose between all the other stuff or sexual fulfillment…I don't want a liar, or someone that doesn't pay attention to me or doesn't care about the family. If I had to choose, I would rather have all that stuff.

Martin: When number one is met, all the other needs are met. Trust me, we are very simple to please.

Chelsea: Then how do we meet each other's needs, when one person must have their need met in order to meet their partner's needs and vice versa?

Martin: So, let's talk about that. Let's walk through that part because this also ties into finances. Her number one top need for financial security is my number two need. Everyone needs to be financially secure, but here's the deal…for me sexual fulfillment trumps everything else.

Chelsea: You'd rather be doing it all the time and not have any money? You'd rather be getting some action than have a home?

Martin: Look, I come from a poor African country with some of the poorest people. They have a bunch of kids there, it's a recreational activity.

So, let's talk about the steps we went through, the steps we are going through right now in terms of meeting each other's needs. And then we will talk about how exactly it ties in with your money. I have a conclusion that I came to and it will help all of us, especially men.

Chelsea: Ok, so this is how things have evolved in our relationship. When we first met, I was living in Las Vegas with William. We moved to San Diego for me to start building my financial business. I had been in the financial industry many years ago, but I was coming back to it. I went to a financial seminar and learned how I needed to earn passive income and become financially free.

At this seminar, I met a group of people who were helping others by educating and empowering them financially. I thought "This is exactly what I need." They said, "Why don't you come out to San Diego and work with us. You can even stay with us. We're getting this big huge house and you can come live with us." I had always wanted to live in San Diego, so after much consideration I decided to go for it.

I get to San Diego and show up to this house. It's huge with a pool, hot tub, built in BBQ, everything. There were a few single people living there all working in the financial industry together and building their dreams. So, who else is there in this house? This guy….that's how we met. I literally showed up at his door.

Martin: So that's the initial start of our relationship. We had this big house; it was like a business house. All these people were going after their dreams. We would entertain people at this house; we would have parties and have a great time in San Diego. Chelsea came there because she wanted to get back in the financial game and that's how things got stirred up. In the very beginning, what was that like for you?

Chelsea: When we met, this was in the summer time, in a beautiful house, beautiful area; all my dreams are coming true. I meet this guy who has the same goals and dreams as me and we start dating. It was all care free in the beginning. I intended on finding work that would allow me to fund building my business, but wasn't working quite yet. We were starting this new life, William was happy to be in San Diego. There was a lot less stress. Then as we started combining our business, becoming a family and combining our finances all these layers of reality started piling on. For me, considering that sexual fulfillment is on the bottom of my list…

Martin: Here's the thing, I didn't have her do this emotional needs quiz in the beginning. So, I thought it was near the top of her list because she was care free and we were having a great time. And I grilled her in the beginning, by the way. I wanted to know if she wanted to have kids and how many. I wasn't messing around; I wanted to know what kind of person she was if I was going to date her. I wanted to know she was the real deal.

Chelsea: So, he thought that's how things would stay. But, there was a turning point. Things went from care free and then all of a sudden finances became stressful for me. I had to get some business going and William was starting a new school and then you wanted date night, which to me was optional. It was one extra thing on my plate and my survival started feeling threatened. I felt like I had to choose between having a boyfriend and being a mom…and something just shut off for me.

It wasn't that he was literally threatening me or forcing me to go out with him, but that's how I felt. So, all of a sudden the care free Chelsea was gone.

Martin: And I'm like "What happened to that girl?"

Chelsea: I put the brakes on big time. I didn't even know if I wanted to be in a relationship anymore. It was just too much for me and I felt too much pressure.

Since then, it has been about trying to work through that and learn about each other's needs.

Well, we obviously stayed together and ended up moving across country. We got married, we're both parents now, and running a business together. We ended up parting ways with our original group and in many ways we were starting over. All of these things just piled one on top of the other and all I could think about was everything we needed to be doing…I was definitely not thinking about sex. Ladies, I'm sure you can relate.

Martin: So let's get to the point of the conflict that's happening right now. So they have some context around the back story.

Chelsea: Ok, so how do we get on the same page? How do we make sure that both of our needs are being met? Well, we had to have a discussion about what financial security means to me and what sexual fulfillment means to you. Because I'm thinking "Ok, well you had this need met here, so does that mean your good to go for a certain period of time?"

Martin: She thinks it's like an oil change. You get one and you're good for 10,000 miles. It's like she thinks I'm good for ninety days, but I need a daily oil change. So here's the issue, we titled our book Let's Fight About Money because it's such a key thing. She needs that for financial stability and it's my number two need.

So, how do we meet each other's emotional needs? There are two things couples fight about most…money and sex. We have put together some steps to deal with this that you can use yourself because I know, if you are a guy, this is happening to you. This is happening to guys all around the world.

Chelsea: Talk about how men's spending habits affect their sex life. This is where the connection is being missed.

Martin: When we sit down with our clients, men tend to be more aggressive and women tend to be more conservative. Women look at money like a pool. It's there and they think it's going to run out. Men tend to look at money like an ocean. It comes in and it flows out. That's how men and women view investments on a general scale.

Chelsea is the saver and I am the spender. I'm not a frivolous spender though; I like to spend on things that will grow our business. But, I never equated how high on her emotional needs scale financial security was, in order for her to meet my top need. I think if I understood it was that important for her and that my top need was on the bottom of her list, trust me I would have moved faster in our business. I would want to save more money.

Chelsea: Man, we should have done this quiz sooner!

Martin: This is how men should look at it; if you save more money, you have more sex. If you change your spending habits, you have more sex. It's all tied together in your relationship and if men can understand financial security is that important to women, I think they will start looking at money differently.

The number one topic men think about is sex and then they think about money. Why do we want to get the money? We look better when we have more money and then we can get intimate.

Chelsea: Here's what happens when the man's need is not met. If he's a spender, maybe he goes and blows some money on himself. That stresses the women out and she feels like he can't be trusted with money. Now, instead of moving closer together, they end up moving farther apart.

For me, when we first started learning about what each other's money habits and personalities are…remember he's a spender and I'm a saver. So, each time he would spend…it's not only based on what's going on in the relationship currently, but it's also based on past experiences and relationships.

In a past relationship, I had a horrible experience with money and trust. So, the fact that Martin was a spender…he was already in the red zone with me. Anytime he spent, or overspent, that was justification for me that I couldn't trust him with money. I felt my financial security was in jeopardy, I was on RED ALERT and that shut off my ability to fulfill his top need.

Martin: The problem is not that Chelsea's top need is financial security and my top need is sexual fulfillment. The problem is that my top need is Chelsea's dead least need. So the first thing I looked at is that I want to make my wife happy and I want to do everything I can to meet her emotional needs. This has to do with resources and business and it dovetails into how your finances are connected. Money is connected to everything. Our mission is to help people transform their lives and we do that by helping them transform their finances.

So, from the very beginning…I'm a Taurus. I don't 100% believe in all that, but I think it's fun.

Chelsea: He's telling you he's stubborn

Martin: Yes, I'm stubborn, Taurus' are also very sensual and we like what we like. We like nice things. We like pretty people, Chelsea is very pretty and when I met her I was extremely attracted to her. Taurus' are also loyal, very loyal.

Chelsea: So are Virgos.

Martin: Virgos are a little boring though.

Chelsea: WHAT!?!

Martin: Virgos are a little boring. Taurus' are exciting. We're fun.

Chelsea: Oh yea, way to get your emotional need met!

Martin: That's not helping me out?

Chelsea: Nope. That's a little check mark for you ;)

Martin: Look, money plays an extremely important role and whether we agree with it or not…guys may not think of it like that. When you are a couple in a relationship, if you focus on meeting each other's needs you win every time because it's not just about you…it's about them. So, I keep asking myself what I need to do to fulfill her top emotional need of financial stability, which comes down to money.

Chelsea: Ok, so as we talked more about this we discovered four golden keys that helped us navigate exactly what to do. If you're in a relationship, first of all, you have to decide that you do want to meet each other's needs, you want to stay in the relationship, and you want each other to be happy. You can't expect your needs to be met if you aren't willing to meet your partner's needs, right?

So, where do we go from here? If my needs have to be met in order to meet yours and your needs have to be met in order to meet mine…who goes first…the chicken or the egg? How do we meet on the same page? Especially when meeting your top need requires more than just going through the motions whether you want to or not or whether you have a million things on your mind or not.

Ok, here's our four golden keys:

1. **Self-Awareness**: You have to first be aware of what your own needs are and in what order, what do they mean to you and how do you know when they are met?

Martin: That's where the quiz came in. That's what helped us become self-aware.

Chelsea: Yes, I started looking at how I communicate my emotional needs? What are my emotional needs and in what order? That's how I found the quiz.

2. **Spouse Awareness**: You have to understand what your partner's emotional needs are, in what order and how to know when they are met. This is very important to know how they are met, because I could think that one day of sexual fulfillment for Martin would be good for him for a week, or he might think that one month of financial security would fulfill my top need.

3. **Decide how bad you want your needs to be met**: This is a great way to start shifting your thinking. If your top need is nowhere to be found on your partner's list or not in the same order, you have to ask yourself how bad do you want your emotional needs to be met.

Being in business together as entrepreneurs, we are constantly taking risks and investing in our business so financial security may mean something completely different to me than it does to him. Just because there's money in the bank and we have our financial future planned out doesn't mean that I feel financially secure.

So, if Martin would have known how important financial security is for me…maybe he would have shifted his thinking because he wants his number one need to be met. Same with me, if financial security is so important to me and I know that fulfilling his need for sexual fulfillment will get my emotional need met…maybe I could get in the mood a little more often. ;)

4. **How to actually meet each other's needs**: It's one thing to talk about it, but how do I actually get into the mood more often? How do I clear my mind of all the things that need to be done? We women always have a million things going on in our mind. I'm thinking about William, our business, this, that, all the things that need to be done and it all has to be cleared out of my mind. So, how do I do that?

We are together most of the time, working on our business, as parents, as a family. Just because we are together doesn't mean we are intimately together all the time. We have to make specific time to focus on our relationship, just Martin and I. It's not time with William or our business. We have to make that time for each other and we have to commit to it.

Martin: So those are the things we decided to do in order to handle this area of disagreement. My goal in life is to take her number ten need and push that up closer to the top! So I need to do what I need to do to be able to fulfill her emotional needs so she can meet my emotional need. Because everything in her case is tied to finances, that makes it an easier target to focus on.

When you are an entrepreneur and you are building your own business, there will be peaks and valleys in your business. So that means whenever you go through a valley and your spouse's top emotional need is financial security, there will be some conflict. This is something that is happening in our real life and we are talking to you about it because our hope is that it helps you in some way to have a conversation with your partner.

It's not always comfortable to talk about some of these kinds of things, but it's not comfortable in your house either. When you talk to your spouse, they may not want to take an emotional needs quiz, they may think it's stupid.

Chelsea: You can look at it like this; we are willing to have this conversation in front of you and everyone else who reads this book. We even talked about it on our Live show in front of over a thousand live viewers. So, hopefully that encourages some of you to have that conversation in the privacy of your own home.

Martin: The end goal that we have is to really help people transform their lives. As a couple and having a financial background, we know this is an area of conflict. We started looking at ourselves and asking what are the areas that we disagree on that we can highlight and share with others. Because we do have these discussions and so many people want to know how we work through all the things we go through in order to have a successful marriage and a successful business.

You wouldn't believe how many people reach out to Chelsea and I and say "I want to learn how you and Chelsea work together in business because I can't get the support of my spouse."

Chelsea: They ask "Do you guys really get along that well?" Not all the time. But, we are committed to making our business successful, being successful parents and having a successful relationship. I want his needs met, just like he wants my needs to be met. So, we have to have these conversations that are going to be uncomfortable. We are not always going to agree.

We have to figure out how to meet each other's needs.

Martin: We have a lot of uncomfortable conversations especially about money. The idea for this book was spurred from disagreements that we had. We take you through what happened, what I was thinking, what Chelsea was thinking and then we have a conversation about it.

Chelsea: We help walk you through exactly how to discover what your beliefs and habits are around money and that also translates to everything else in your life. Depending on the way you were raised, what you saw, what you heard and what you experienced all make up who you are today and how you see the world. You only see the world through your eyes.

So, first you have to understand how you see the world, how you behave, what you think and believe. Then, you have to understand that your partner sees the world through their own eyes. Then, you can figure out what is the same, what is different and how you can work together. As long as you love each other, are committed to each other, want to make the relationship work and for each other to be happy…there is always somewhere positive to go from there.

If you can't get passed that, then you may have more serious problems in your relationship. You've got to at least have a commitment to each other and it all starts from understanding yourself.

Martin: So where it goes from here is that I am intently focused on creating financial security, not just because it's Chelsea top need. One of the things that I started to do is to track more and more things in our business as it relates to our money. We have some big goals and the thing for me to keep in mind is that when we have valleys in our business, it causes stress for Chelsea and that impacts her being able to meet my top emotional need.

I have a better understanding of it now, because when I am stressed, I want my top need met to relieve that pressure. Chelsea sees it the same way, but we have different needs that must be met to relieve the pressure.

Chelsea: You were thinking about that care free Chelsea, before we became a family, a business, a marriage and all the pressures of life started piling on.

Martin: I got thrown for a loop. I was wondering what happened to that person. I'm thinking I'm all in, I like her, start dating her, ran through all the questions I had, she answered all my questions right and passed my test. Then, she flipped on me a little bit.

This emotional needs quiz has really helped us a whole lot.

Chelsea: Here's something funny that Martin thought about marriage...he thought that whatever happens before marriage, is just accentuated after marriage. So, if you got a lot of action before marriage...he thought there would be that much more. For me, and I think a majority of women, it's the complete opposite.

Martin: Yea, I thought as you got to know each other better and learned what each other likes, it would get better and better and more often.

Action to take:

1. Take the quiz here: **Bit.ly/EmotionalNeeds**

2. Invite your partner to take the quiz.

3. Share your top 5 needs with each other and why they are important to you.

4. Without judgement or criticism, talk about some ways you can meet each other's top needs and start putting it into action.

For more resources and accountability go to: **LetsFightAboutMoney.com**

Chapter 7:

What Will Your Legacy Be? Bills or Benefits?

Why teaching kids good money habits became my mission

Chelsea: When our son William started school, I began to see the very same issues that I struggled with growing up. I just didn't fit into the cookie cutter lesson plans…and as I grew up, I found out that what you need to learn to be successful isn't even taught in school.

> *Kids don't learn about good money habits, or how to develop their natural skills, or discover their passions, and they certainly don't learn about starting their own business.*

School had not changed, since the beginning of its time, from expecting kids to just be quiet, sit still, not speak out, do as they are told and to all learn the same way for the ultimate goal of preparing them to become employees.

Let me give you an example. William has a real passion for art, and he's great at it! One day in first-grade art class, he was really into a project. He was so into it that he didn't hear the teacher announce it was time to clean up, and she had asked several times. She soon became very frustrated, and William got into trouble. So, what do you think his punishment was?

Well, William was struggling with reading at the time. He just wasn't very interested in it. We were working with him to try and find things he was interested in that he would enjoy reading about. I was so proud when he found a book he liked, and he asked his teacher if he could read it to the class. He was really excited and was going to read it that day. But, because he didn't clean up in art, his punishment was that he didn't get to read to the class that day. The very thing we were encouraging him to do got taken away and the thing he loves to do, he got in trouble for doing.

I couldn't understand this reasoning. I wondered what it was teaching him. That if he focuses too much on what he is passionate about, he will get into trouble and that it's not worth trying to improve himself because it can just be taken away?

I didn't want that to be William's future. I didn't want him to give up on his dreams before he even had a chance to know what they were really. I didn't want him to settle for a job when he got older, just to pay the bills, and I certainly didn't want him to make the same financial mistakes I made growing up.

I wanted to teach him by example how to live a happy, healthy, successful, passionate, fun and fulfilling life that he could develop and share his gifts to make a major impact in the world.

That meant I had to figure it out for myself...But how?

For seven years I struggled as a single mom, feeling like I had to choose between financial success and family success. I knew there were other moms out there looking for a better way and if I could figure it out for myself, I could help them figure it out too. So,

I set out on a journey to learn about good money habits, how to earn passive income and become financially free living my passions.

I did a lot of work on my mindset, beliefs, actions and ultimately my habits. I met some people in the Financial Industry, and I saw an opportunity to educate and empower myself, teach William good money habits and help other families to do the same.

Since then, I met Martin and together we have built a business teaching personal and financial development. William, now 11, has two businesses that earn passive income and one of them teaches kids good money habits.

All of the things I began to imagine, many years ago, have now become our reality.

We are on a mission to help as many families create the lives they dream of and to do that, it takes money!

I began to think about what kind of man I wanted William to become. We reflect on what kind of partner, business or life we want…but how often do we think about what kind of adult we want our kids to become? It's hard to think about our little angels growing up, but we aren't raising them to be kids, we are raising them to become adults.

So, the question remains…what kind of adult do you want to raise?

I believe that most parents want the very best for their kids. But what if we could equip them for even more?

What if we could teach them the value of money, how to make their own, what to do with it and how to use it to make a difference?

The beliefs and habits that we instill into our children from the beginning of their life are what shapes them into the people they become and the impact that they can make.

Write down the qualities you want your child to have and then you know who you have to become to teach them by example.

Mindset

When talking about good money habits, we must talk about mindset. It's not enough to just know how to make money and what to do with it, but

The relationship we have with money will absolutely determine our financial future.

We all developed certain beliefs about money, depending on the experiences we had growing up.

For example, if money was scarce, you may have heard things like "Money doesn't grow on trees" or "We can't afford that." You may have grown up believing money will leave you, and so, you became a fearful saver. On the other hand; if money was abundant, you might have heard things like "It's only money" or "You can't take it with you." You may have grown up believing money should be spent freely, and so, you became a frivolous spender.

Here's another example…when a child gets their first dollar, maybe from you or an aunt or uncle or grandparent, what is the first thing that child is told? "Go spend it!" What does the child do? Exactly what they are told, they go spend it…all of it. From their very first experience with money, they learn to blow it all. Most of the time, when children get money, they get really excited and spend it all without even thinking about it. When they ask for you to buy them something, they don't think about the cost, or if it's in the budget,

Kids don't understand the value of money unless we teach it to them.

But how can we teach them the value of money if we were never taught? Imagine if you had learned good money habits as a kid?

How would your life be different if you learned good money habits from the very first dollar you ever got a hold of?

What dreams could you have accomplished that you still haven't been able to? At what age did you start giving up on your dreams because your parents told you that you couldn't do it, or it was time to grow up, or there just wasn't enough money? Imagine if money was never the issue and you had all the resources at your disposal to create all your dreams? And along with all of those resources, you also learned how to earn your own money, save your own money and even invest your own money!

What mistakes would you have been able to avoid? Could you have avoided getting a high-interest payday loan, student debt that maybe you are still trying to pay off, or maybe it was a bankruptcy? We've all made some financial mistakes. But, imagine if you could have avoided them, where would your life be now?

That's what you can give your kids.

Where Do You Start?

What example are you setting now? We must always start with ourselves. If you don't have good money habits, how will you teach your kids? And even if you could teach them good money habits, without having them yourself, it won't stick because they will learn more by watching what you do. You know the saying "Do as I say, not as I do?" Well, I think we can agree that it doesn't work.

What are you teaching your kids about money now?
Have you talked to them about money? What do you
communicate about money? Do your kids see you buying
a lot of extra things, or do you talk about how tight money
is? Everything you do and say is soaked up by our little
sponges.

What are you not teaching your kids about money now?
Is money a topic not talked about in your house? That is
the reality for so many families out there. In fact, many
parents are more comfortable talking about sex and drugs
with their kids than they are talking about money. I have
also seen many kids have everything done for them and
paid for them, that when they move out on their own, they
have no idea how to do anything for themselves.

Parents often think they are helping their kids, but they are
actually robbing them of the chance to make small
mistakes and learn along the way. And now the mistakes
are much bigger. They don't know how to pay bills, or
balance a checkbook, or create a budget. If they never
learned the key milestones along the way, it can be super
overwhelming, and, they can start to get into some serious
trouble very quickly.

Practical teaching tips

Here are some things you can start doing now. Create age-
appropriate responsibilities with the following goals in
mind:

- Help your kids understand the value of money and how much things cost

- Let them make spending decisions with extra money you would normally spend on them

- Give them opportunities to earn money. Incentivize them to learn about mindset, money, and success.

For example: pay them to read success books such as:
> Secrets of The Millionaire Mind by T. Harv Eker
> Keys to Success for Kids by Caleb Maddix
> Kids 4 Wealth by William …coming soon!

- Help them figure out what things they enjoy doing and how they can monetize it

For example: write a book or create a business

- Go to **Kids4Wealth.Com** to get our son William's video where he teaches the easiest money system for kids.

Are you & your spouse on the same page?

If you are in a relationship or parenting together, it is EXTREMELY important to be on the same page in many areas…especially when it comes to money! As we talked about earlier, it's important to know your money beliefs and your partner's as well.

This topic is critical to a successful relationship, yet many couples just don't talk about it. Even though *it affects us every day of our entire life, the fun things we get to say yes to and the difficult things we have to say no to.*

Martin and I went to a John Maxwell conference and there was something John said that really stood out to me. He said, "*Sometimes people are more comfortable with old problems than they are with new solutions.*" I believe the real issue is that people have not been educated or empowered financially even to know what options they have, or how it could affect their financial future. This is why Martin and I are dedicated to the changing Financial Literacy.

It takes work, communication, and commitment to be on the same page when it comes to money and relationships, but the payoff is so worth it!

While it's crucial to teach our kids the tools to have good money habits, as I talked about earlier, *they will learn more about what they see, hear and experience.* So, if they see you and your partner fighting about money, or not talking about money at all…that will absolutely factor into their money beliefs which lead to their habits.

If you are still asking yourself "Do I really need to teach my kids about money?" Consider these questions…

What happens if you don't teach your kids good money habits? What are you taking away from them? Everything…you are robbing them of the freedom of having choices. You are setting them up to be taken advantage of and pushed around. You are dooming them to have to shrink their dreams to fit the size of their reality. You could be ruining their life…and yours! Think about it, if your kids never learn good money habits, they could be financially dependent on you…FOREVER!

What happens if you do teach your kids good money habits? What are you giving them? Everything…you are giving them the tools to have options, the freedom and confidence to make their own decisions, the chance to make their dreams come true, to contribute in their own community and even the world.

I'll give you an example of how teaching William good money habits helped him to become confident and independent with more than just his money. We wanted to teach William the value of money and help him develop good buying habits. So, we told him we would buy all of his necessities but he had to buy anything extra that he wanted, except for holidays or special occasions. He has always loved Legos and he is excellent at building them, so as his skill improved so did the price of the sets he wanted.

I took him to the store one day when he wanted to buy some new Legos. He brought his money and was super excited until he started looking at the prices. He said "Man Legos are expensive! Why do they have to cost so much?" We talked a little bit about supply and demand, and then he continued the search for a Lego set that fit his budget of only about $11. The closest he could find was a set for $14, and he said to me "Well, maybe I can ask if they will accept the amount of money I have." My first thought was to say "No, this is Walmart…it doesn't get much cheaper than that." But then I thought, who am I to tell him no? I like to find the lesson in everything, so this could be a great lesson in him hearing a "No."

We went up to the register and William showed the cashier how much money he had and asked if they could make an exception. The cashier said she would have to ask the manager, so she called him over. As he walked up, the cashier explained the situation. He turned to William, looked at him, looked at his money and asked: "How much money do you have?" William showed him. "You saved that all by yourself?" He asked. "Yes!" William answered. To my absolute shock, he agreed to lower the price to the amount William had and even waived the tax. William learned about taxes on another shopping trip.

I was the one that learned the lesson that day…not one lesson, but two!

1. It never hurts to ask
2. Always negotiate

Teaching Kids About Money: A Dad's Perspective

I'd like to ask a simple question, ***"What does it mean to be a dad?"***

While the question itself is simple, it has such a complicated answer. It is my hope that as you discover this answer for yourself if you haven't already, you'll recognize both the joy and awesome responsibility of this role.

When I think about my own dad, two words come to mind… Protector and Provider. As a child, I looked to him for protection and provision. He was a good father, always attempting to make sure his family was taken care of.

Maybe you had a dad like mine. Someone who encouraged you, shared his wisdom and helped you discover your place in the world. Or perhaps you didn't have that. Maybe your dad wasn't around or maybe he caused you to question your place in the world rather than find it.

I don't know what kind of dad you had, but I know what kind of dad you are or can be. By asking yourself that simple question, "What does it mean to be a dad?" you're already headed in the right direction.

When we get married, it's very common for your spouse and your children to take on your last name. This symbolizes unity and should spark a sense of passing something on to the next generation. First, you pass on your name, then perhaps your knowledge, your beliefs, your habits and eventually your possessions.

This chapter serves as a guide to help you raise successful and well-adjusted adults. This portion will teach you how to educate your child(ren) financially coming from a dad's point of view. Before we get into the specifics, it's important to have the right frame of mind on this topic.

So, here's another important question for you... *What will your legacy be?*

Throughout England's history, the family property passed down to the oldest male child. Althorp, the childhood residence of Princess Diana has been in their family for 19 generations and her family has lived there for over 500 years.

In the United States, we wouldn't dare think of disinheriting daughters just because of their gender but there was one benefit of the English system. It was that since parents already knew which child would inherit what is left behind, they started teaching them how to be good stewards at a young age.

They were prepared for their adult responsibilities when they were children. When your children become adults, they'll have adult responsibilities to deal with. They have to make many of the same financial decisions you have to deal with.

Things like having a budget, getting a loan or mortgage, dealing with debt, saving for retirement, paying for college, protecting the family's assets from loss and if done properly, passing on what's left to the next generation.

Maybe your parents didn't teach you about money. Mine didn't either. We can allow the cycle to continue or we can take charge and break that cycle once and for all. So our challenge to you is this, think about your children as future stewards for what you'll leave them. And since they'll be your stewards, shouldn't they learn to be good ones like those English families?

Who is responsible for teaching them good financial habits? YOU ARE! If in your household, the dad is considered the leader, then you must accept the responsibility to lead your children to great habits in all areas of life, including their finances.

If you're like most dads out there, your parents likely did not teach you about money. But that is no excuse to allow the cycle to continue. If it doesn't start with you, then WHO? If you don't start now, then WHEN?

If you realize something is important and you don't how to do it… learn. Here are some practical steps to take.

1. Commit

When I was about 12 years old, my father made me a very important proposition. He said that once a week he wanted me to make a short list of items my younger brother Tony needed help with. He was 9 at the time. I'll admit that I did not want the responsibility and I tried to get out of it. My father explained the importance of this responsibility and after he had spoken with me, I gave him my commitment to follow through.

I kept that promise… *for about two weeks!* I went back to my dad and told him that my brother was often difficult to deal with and I wanted out of my commitment. He smiled and said, "Martin, so you would like to give up and walk away from the commitment you made?"

Well, when you put it that way! He went on to explain to me that when you make a commitment, there will be times when it may seem difficult to keep that commitment but you must stick to it. When you have children, helping them acquire the skills they need in life including how to handle money requires a commitment from you. Before anything happens, you must commit!

2. Learn

From birth, your learning journey begins. You come into this world screaming and crying and soon you learn who's there to comfort you. Your mother holds you close, flashes a smile and you feel the connection to the woman who carried you for nine months.

You learn to sit and you learn to crawl. You learn to speak and stand and take your first steps. You learn to read and write and eventually, you learn to drive.

And even though everyone has been learning since birth, most of them slow down on that learning journey when they become an adult. Many even stop learning and just remain stagnant. This cannot and will not be you. By picking up this book, you have an interest in learning and we challenge you to learn more about how money works so you can teach your children.

As parents, we desperately want our children to do what we SAY. Just remember that what we DO rings so loudly in their ears. With 2 out of 3 adults financially illiterate worldwide, you have to learn things yourself to break that cycle.

Here are some key things you should learn and understand for yourself. Learn about the importance of having a spending plan AKA a budget. If you don't use one, we have resources that can help you in that area.

Learn about interest and how money grows. According to the Federal Reserve Bank, 65% of American adults do not understand how compound interest works. Our son William learned about earning and paying interest before he was ten years old. He learned those things because WE learned about them.

3. Teach

My father, who was my hero, passed away a few years ago. I still remember the life lessons he taught me. Sometimes it may not appear like your kids are listening to the instructions you give them, but trust me, they're watching. You teach your children by what you say but mostly by what you DO. Yes, at times they might sigh or roll their eyes, but they will thank you later! Find ways to incorporate financial lessons in life. A great way to teach them is when you're at the store, and they want you to buy them something.

We have a popular video online titled "Buying Nutella On Credit." William LOVES Nutella. He will put that hazelnut treat on anything, including eggs. He loves Nutella so much that he chooses to buy it with his own money. During a Costco trip one day, William forgot the money for his Nutella. He budgeted for it and was ready to purchase it when he remembered that he left his money at home.

William asked to borrow some money from us to get it. We used this opportunity to teach him a very important lesson about debt and negotiation. I started filming on my phone when Chelsea told him that he would have to pay interest on the money he wanted to buy Nutella.

In his desire for Nutella, William quickly accepted the offer. I then asked him if he thought the interest was fair. He thought about it and started to negotiate with Chelsea. He was able to get a lower interest rate on his loan.

As adults, we're often excited by the item we want to buy and often fail to see the true cost of it. Many adults never negotiate an interest rate; they just pay what is asked of them. By teaching William these things at a young age, we help him develop and reinforce good financial habits. Would your life be different if you learned good money habits at William's age or even younger?

4. Monitor

Lastly, pay attention to their progress. William would often tell us how many of his friends never had any money because they spent it all. He shares examples of how much money his friends waste on things they don't need just because they have the money.

Keep a close eye on whether or not your kids are learning and applying the lessons they're learning from you. Sometimes we'll ask William to calculate the tax on an item he wants to purchase, and he'll pull out his phone and use the calculator.

There is perhaps no greater joy as a parent than when your child understands and uses something you've taught them. It reassures you that maybe you're not doing such a bad job after all.

What do you want for your kids and their financial future?

Action to take:

1. What are you teaching your kids now about money?

2. What do you want to teach them about money?

3. What kind of adults do you want your kids to become?

4. What do you need to learn, do or stop doing to be that example?

5. Go to **Kids4Wealth.com** and purchase William's video for your kids or someone else's.

Take the time to answer each question for yourself and then without judgment, share your answers with each other and talk about how you can get on the same page, if you aren't already.

For more resources and accountability go to: **LetsFightAboutMoney.com**

Chapter 8:

How These 6 Building Blocks Lead to An Unbreakable Financial House

Many people can feel overwhelmed by all the things they have to do for their finances, so we've broken down your financial house into six manageable building blocks:

1. Cash Flow

2. Debt Management

3. Emergency Fund

4. Proper Protection

5. Build Wealth

6. Preserve Wealth

We'll look at each building block individually but they all work together to build a strong and unbreakable financial house. If one block is weak, it threatens the entire financial house.

Start by working on your Mind Set:

> Changing your thinking from "**budget**," which is restrictive and you don't have control of to "**spending plan**," where you are in control of how your money is spent. You are empowered.

Building Block One:
CASH FLOW

1. *Track your spending:*

- ➢ Know what's coming in & going out. Keep your receipts, especially if you own your own business
- ➢ **Mint.com** is a great tool for tracking & budgeting.
  - ▪ You can link all of your bank accounts and even loans together to see everything in one place.
  - ▪ It categorizes purchases for you and tells you how much you are spending in each area (house, car, food, misc., etc.).
  - ▪ It will even help you set goals for saving or paying down debt.

2. *Set up separate bank accounts:*

Expenses: know the difference between "Needs & Wants." Can you live without it or do you need it to survive? Examples of Needs are Mortgage/Rent, Utilities, Car/Maintenance, Food, and Insurance. You may have business expenses like Phones, Internet, Office, etc. Some examples of Wants are: Starbucks, Eating Out, Going Out, Buying a New car when yours is just fine. These are not always going to be the same for everyone. This is a great place to start teaching kids good money habits. It's very important for them to learn the value of money and learning the difference between Needs & Wants is an essential part of that!

Emergency Savings: We all hate having emergencies, especially when we don't properly plan for them. Having an emergency fund can make the difference between going into debt vs. not going into debt. For example, we get a flat tire and don't have the extra money to pay for it. What do we do? Either charge it to a credit card or use money that was for other expenses and get behind on something else. It's a never ending cycle that you just can't seem to get out of. It seems that the more unprepared we are for emergencies, the more we have. But, the more prepared we are, not only do we appear to have less, they don't seem as bad because we are prepared financially.

Long Term Savings: For big purchase/trips/holidays. We use this one for multiple things:

We use it year round for holidays & birthdays. This way we don't have to take money out of our expense account, we save a little bit all through the year and not only does it add up but helps us from overspending too.

You can also use this account for Trips & Vacations, big purchases like a car or down payment on a house, etc.

Fun: The best account of all. Just like it sounds, it's for FUN. No judgments. Each family member gets to spend their amount of fun money any way they want. This is where you get to think in abundance and splurge!

Taxes: if you own your own business: The great thing about owning your own business is that taxes are not taken out of your income. But, you do eventually have to pay them, so put your money where it can work for you before you give it to the government.

Business: if you own your own: You need money to operate your business, whether it's a small business and you have a home office or you have employees and overhead. Never combine your business and personal money, this can cause major problems on both sides!

Building Block Two:
DEBT MANAGEMENT

1. ***Spend less than you make***. It sounds like common sense, but you would be surprised at how many people we meet who are spending more than they earn and are just getting deeper in debt. Here are a few things to think about when it comes to debt:

2. ***Learn about the Rule of 72*** here: **Bit.ly/Rof72** and how it can make a HUGE impact on your financial fitness. You must know the rate your debt is growing if you ever plan on paying it off.

3. ***Mint.com*** is a great tool for viewing, tracking and managing all of your debt. You can even set goals to pay it off and figure out how long it will take.

4. ***CreditKarma.com*** is another great tool for debt. This site will track your credit score, tell you what areas are negatively impacting it and give you suggestions to improve. They also suggest different credit cards that would give you the best options for your score level. Credit cards are not all bad and some give great benefits if you can manage your

spending plan properly and not be tempted to overspend, which is easier said than done!

5. *Are you sure you have the right mortgage?* And, do you know why it may not be in your best interest to pay it off early?

6. *Are still paying off student loans?* Do you want your kids to do the same? Is there a better way?

7. *Should you buy or lease your car?*

Building Block Three:
EMERGENCY FUND

This can be a make or break for your family as we mentioned in the Cash Flow Building Block. We all hate emergencies, especially when we aren't prepared for them. Somehow when we are prepared, emergencies don't seem as big.

This has so much to do with our mindset. If we stress about emergencies and focus on them, that's what we attract. However, when we are not stressed about it, we find that out of sight is out of mind.

Start saving a little each month, in a separate account and you will be surprised how fast it will add up!

Building Block Four:
PROPER PROTECTION

It's not something we like to think about, but what would happen to your family if you were to die?

Would they be able to stay in your current home?

Would your spouse have to go right back to work?

Would your kids be able to stay in their current school?

What if you didn't die, but got sick or hurt and couldn't work?

Without your income plus additional medical costs, how long could you maintain your current lifestyle?

There is no greater gift than protecting the ones you love!

Building Block Five:
BUILD WEALTH

Is your money working for you?

Could it be working harder?

We want to grow what we have worked hard to build and save. It's important to learn strategies to create wealth & protect yourself from losses along the way. Seek advice from a qualified professional who can create a plan to fit your specific needs. If you don't already have one, reach out to us at the link below.

Building Block Six:
PROTECT WEALTH

What kind of legacy do you want to leave?

Have you taken steps to ensure those wishes will be met?

If you don't have the right documents in place, make sure to talk with a professional who can help you put together what you need. If you don't already have one, reach out to us at the link below.

We strive to build a life we love and leave something to the next generation.

To print a PDF copy of the 6 Blocks go to: **Bit.ly/6Blocks**

For more resources and accountability go to: **LetsFightAboutMoney.com**

Now What?

We hope you have enjoyed this book, but even more, we genuinely hope that you will apply what we have shared with you to transform your relationship, your finances and your life.

It wasn't easy sharing some of the more difficult times in our relationship, but the fact that we discovered the tools to not only work through them, but to truly create a life we love together. The thought of being able to help even just one couple out there to do the same, made it all worth it.

So let's recap what you learned in this book…

In Chapter 1, you learned why people fight about money and discovered that most of the time it has nothing to do with the actual conflict at hand. You must learn about your own relationship with money before you can understand your partner's and definitely before you can resolve any conflicts.

In Chapter 2, we talked about why it's so important for both partners to understand and communicate about their current financials as well as future goals and plans. Nobody wants to be left in the dark.

In Chapter 3, we revealed how different money personalities affect your every decision and why you must learn what yours is if you ever want to have control over your money decisions.

In Chapter 4, you discovered that self-reflection is the only sure way to change an environment, even if your partner doesn't want to change.

In Chapter 5, we share exactly how to stop fighting each other and start fighting for each other, so you can truly become an unstoppable power couple.

In chapter 6, you may have heard for the very first time that your financial security and sexual fulfillment are directly linked together. We showed you how to get more of both. Who doesn't want that?

In Chapter 7, we gave you practical tools to teach your kids good money habits and how to set the right example, so they don't have to read this book in the future. ;)

And in Chapter 8, after you learned how to communicate with each other effectively, we actually show you exactly what to do with your money to build and Unbreakable Financial House and truly live the life you want.

We encourage you to take each action we laid out specifically for you in each chapter as they build on each other. Reading this book is a great start, but it's the actions that will absolutely transform your life.

Sometimes that's easier said than done, right? Well, we want you to have the success in your relationship and finances that we've been able to create using the exact tools that we shared with you in this book. We want to help you put them into action with encouragement and accountability.

To do this, we have created something VERY special for you: go to **LetsFightAboutMoney.com/free** right NOW! There you will find a video series sharing three secrets from this book that we used to transform our life. This is our gift to you and it also introduces our Let's Fight About Money course where we take you through each section of this book and actually help you apply it to your life.

There are so many other cool things there just for you, so what are you waiting for? See you there!

Love,
Martin & Chelsea